LAYERS

poems by

Prabha Nayak Prabhu

Finishing Line Press
Georgetown, Kentucky

LAYERS

For My Parents
(Prema and Nagendra Nayak)

Copyright © 2019 by Prabha Nayak Prabhu
ISBN 978-1-63534-874-3 First Edition
All rights reserved under International and Pan-American Copyright Conventions.
No part of this book may be reproduced in any manner whatsoever without written permission from the publisher, except in the case of brief quotations embodied in critical articles and reviews.

ACKNOWLEDGMENTS

My sincere thanks to the publications in which the following poems first appeared, sometimes in a slightly altered form or with a different title.

Philadelphia Poets ~ (Con)fusion; Batting for Bats; Zealous Azaleas; Overlooked; Tough Choices; Intertwined; Lonely Leaf's Lament; Silent Treatment; Attention Seeker; Role Reversal
The Sylvan ~ Annual Folly; Enigmatic Union; Light Capers; Self Inflicted Conflict
Ethnic Voices ~ Yesteryears Recalled; Color Coding; Layers
Pennessence: Haiku, Limericks
Poetry Ink ~ In the Shadows; Glimmer of Hope; Transmutation
Mad Poets Review ~ Cell Replacement; Creative Bankruptcy
The Fox Chase Review ~ Deep Rooted
Schuylkill Valley Journal ~ Reflections
Selfhood: Varieties of Experience ~ Networking

Publisher: Leah Maines
Editor: Christen Kincaid
Cover Art: Prabha Nayak Prabhu
Author Photo: Giri Prabhu
Cover Design: Leah Huete

Printed in the USA on acid-free paper.
Order online: www.finishinglinepress.com
also available on amazon.com

Author inquiries and mail orders:
Finishing Line Press
P. O. Box 1626
Georgetown, Kentucky 40324
U. S. A.

Table of Contents

I:
- Zealous Azaleas 1
- Light Capers 2
- Attention Seeker 3
- Ode to Dandelions 4
- Overlooked 5
- Annual Folly 6

II:
- Power of Conviction 7
- Tough Choices 8
- Con(fusion) 9
- Color Coding 10
- Yesteryears Recalled 11
- Deep Rooted 12

III:
- Creative Bankruptcy 13
- Futile Effort 14
- Self-Inflicted Conflict 15
- Haiku 16
- Limericks 17

IV:
- Intertwined 18
- Enigmatic Union 19
- Cell Replacement 20
- Lonely Leaf's Lament 21
- Silent Treatment 22

V:
- Batting for Bats 23
- Role Reversal 24
- In the Shadows 25
- Transmutation 27
- Reflections 28

Insidious Changes	29
Cutting Edge Technology	30
Glimmer of Hope	31
Layers	32
Networking	33
Looking Back	34
Dust to Dust	35
Stirring the Pot	36

I

Zealous Azaleas

Only the other day they seemed intent
on keeping a distance
between themselves,
these young azalea bushes
distinct in shape, size and color.
Some, diffident like young lads
conscious of their stubble,
a few reminiscent of adolescent girls
secretly trying on makeup
for the first time
in a department store,
the early bloomers unabashedly
displaying their beauty.

Who knew they would make
a secret pact
to somehow reach out
and help one another?
bring out the best in each other?
create something
bigger than themselves?

Today I see no space between them
only a riot of colors
each one different ,
yet part of the whole,
a beautiful tapestry
tightly woven.

Light Capers

I stand by the window
and watch
fireflies weaving
fluorescent patterns
in the darkness,
the moon playing
<catch me if you can>
with the clouds,
the stars fluttering
their eyelashes
at invisible admirers.

Yet, when the brightest star
known to man
shines in all its glory,
with the promise of
a myriad wondrous sights
I pull down the blinds
to protect
my newly upholstered furniture.

Attention Seeker

A pair of bright purple
and black wings
flaps away
on the large globe of yellow
mums on my doorstep.
I am intrigued.
Fall is not butterfly season.

Moving closer I see
a leaf that has somehow
managed to escape
from its group
which now carpets the lawn.
Likely hidden from view
while still on the tree
it wanted to be noticed
albeit for a brief period.

So as it was falling
to the ground
the poor thing folded itself
in two and settled in a place
where it could be
the cynosure of all eyes
each time it fluttered
in the wind.
.

I'm tempted to throw away
the truant leaf each time
I water the mums.
Then I think perhaps
I shouldn't deprive it of
its few days of glory.

I leave it alone.

Ode to Dandelions

Harbinger of spring, you bring
the first touch of color
to the ground.
In the emerald grass you shine
like a dainty topaz earring.
Aware that they are no match
to your rich yellow tone,
daffodils, buttercups, sunflowers
forsythias wait until they think
you have come and gone
before they arrive on the scene.
Alas, much to their dismay
you somehow manage to give
them tough competition by
raising your lovely little head
every now and then

How dare people call you a pesky weed!
Don't they know your leaves are
filled with nutrition?
Your forebears were brought here
on ships from Europe for your
culinary and medicinal properties.

You are both dandy and lionhearted
holding out gallantly against all odds
until the cruel blades of the lawn mower
behead you and the pesticide destroys
all chances of your resurgence.

But I shall not cry.

I know you won't let me down.
You will no doubt be back
at the appointed time next year
when my eyes can once again
feast on your beauty.

Overlooked

At daybreak young and
old crowd the trails
around the lake.

Hassled homemakers centered
on their daily chores
follow the same old route
while they try to keep track
of dates and days of the week.

Youngsters in designer sports gear
carry on endless conversations
on their cell phones and plan
their dream home
while they jog.

Retired folks take a break,
relax on benches and reminisce
about their working lives,
feel sad that the good old days
will never come back.

The sun breaks through the clouds
covers the lake in a sheet
of glimmering light.
Branches of the *bougainvillea*
begin their seductive dance moves.

Swarms of chirpy sparrows
swoop down on the grass.
The *koel* perched on a mango tree
entices with its song.

Sadly, no matter young or old
few pay heed to
the sights and sounds
of the here and now.

ANNUAL FOLLY

You are never satisfied with your looks
That is why every fall you try out
all the colorful attire you can find
to make yourself
the cynosure of all eyes.

You succeed in your effort.
Who can be oblivious to such beauty?
I can see you preening yourself
each time you hear someone
sing your praises.
Sadly, while flush with all the adulation,
you forget about your jealous admirer,
the rapacious wind
who disrobes you
and leaves you
standing naked,
s h i v e r i n g
in the cold winter months
until good hearted spring decides
to clothe you again.

Why do you embarrass yourself
year after year?
Why don't you realize
you're beautiful as you are?

II

Power of Conviction

As I watch tabloids promising juicy bits
about the battle over a celebrity's estate
disappear in no time from shelves
at the checkout counter of a supermarket
I'm somehow transported to my childhood.
My Dad's words <*You don't deserve
the money you don't earn*> which he
often repeated begin to ring in my ears.
He didn't merely say these words
he acted on them.

When Grandfather bequeathed the huge
family mansion in his hometown to him,
Dad wanted to donate it to charity.
Opposition and ultimately pressure
from his siblings forced him to sell it
and give each his share.

On his deathbed many years later
I saw Dad put pen to paper.
<*I'm writing a short letter*> he said.
Shortly thereafter he was gone.

In the last letter he ever wrote
Dad donated the entire amount
he had received as his share from
the sale of Grandfather's house
along with the interest accrued
over the years to a children's charity.

I'm so proud of you, Dad!
You didn't just talk the talk
You walked the walk.

Tough Choices
    (For my brother Prakash)

Birthdays, weddings
celebrations planned
ahead of time.

Unexpected deaths
other tragedies occur.

What should one do?
Cancel the events?
Envelope oneself in gloom?

Or

Should one go ahead
and celebrate life?

But what about guilt pangs?
Can they be erased by
a moment of silence
observed in honor of
the departed soul
before the festivities begin?

Hard questions
Even harder answers.

Life goes on . . .

(Con)fusion

Am I on *Mahatma Gandhi Road* or Montgomery Avenue?
People are driving on the left of the road
It must be the former.

Am I eating *masala dosa* or chicken marsala?
There is the distinct taste of oregano
It must be the latter.

Am I listening to Mahler or *Raag Malhar*?
There is no drone instrument in the background
It must be the former.

Am I in Mullica Hill or Malleswaram?
I get the heady scent of fresh *mallige* (jasmine)
It must be the latter.

Straddling two worlds and attempting fusion
often results in confusion.

Color Coding

I pass by houses every morning.
The brick house with the red door
reminds me of Mom's brown sari
with the red border.
The pale yellow house
with the blue windows
reminds me of Mom's yellow sari
with the blue motifs.
The white house
with the green shingles
reminds me of Mom's white sari
with the green checks.

I see colors all the time.
Why do I only think of Mom's saris
when I look at houses?

Today, I finally have the answer.
These are not just houses
they are homes.
Each one of them is a home
someone's home.
When I think of home,
I think of Mom
and when I think of Mom,
I think of her saris.

Sadly, what was once home
ten thousand miles away,
is now just a house
and Mom, a gazillion miles away
is now only a memory.

Mystery solved, reality accepted,
I walk back to the house
that is now home.

Yesteryears Recalled

Happy Diwali says the message
in the **Inbox**.

Diwali, the Festival of Lights
that celebrates the victory of good
over evil, light over darkness.
I am transported in an instant
to my hometown removed
in time and space from
the City of Brotherly Love.

The vibrant tableau unfolds.
Mom's constant nagging to get
up early and be ready for the day
before sunrise—*it's auspicious.*
Prayers, gifts and blessings from elders.
Dad's advice to always do the right thing.
Nonstop eating, endless cups of tea
Friends, neighbors, relatives
all dressed in colorful festive clothes
exchange sweets, wish each other well.
Differences are put on hold for a day.

Then the night! Countless clay oil lamps
with handmade cotton wool wicks
illuminate doorsteps and garden walls
valiantly defying the spoilsport wind.
We kids laugh and scream as we have
the time of our lives with firecrackers.

Grateful for this virtual audio visual treat
I hit **Reply** and type
Happy Diwali.

Deep Rooted

Branches of family
break away
move on.
Older members retire
to old folks' homes.

The <*For Sale*> sign
on the lawn
changes to <*Sold*>

Possessions are hurriedly packed
most discarded
The U-Haul truck turns the corner
No one cares to take
one last look
at the house
that was once home.
Memories, associations
have no worth

The old oak
in the front yard
its branches severed
stands steadfast
in its place.

It only knows one home.

III

Creative Bankruptcy
    (Mono rhyme Octave)

While at the pub my thirst to slake,
I see men fools of themselves make
Regardless of what is at stake.
O'er this into a poem I break,
When at night I stay wide awake.
But despite all the pains I take,
My words sound so hollow and fake.
I'll never be a William Blake.

Futile Effort
    (Minute Poem)

I'll never be a William Blake
My words sound fake
I know that I'm
not good at rhyme.

Iambic meter makes me cry.
Why do I try
creating verse?
I'm never terse.

My Muse is always on the run
has endless fun
deserting me.
I think I'll flee.

Self-Inflicted Conflict

Sometimes it seems a waste of time
sweating over rhythm and rhyme.
It would be nice to go shopping
or perhaps even pub hopping.
Anything to boost my morale
releasing me from my corral.

Yet, when despite stupid urges
a poem finally emerges,
I think it's not bad after all
to sometimes heed the Muse's call.

Haiku

1.
bare trees in winter
woman shorn of beauty weeps
green leaves sprout in spring

2.
snowflakes caressing
my eyelids render me blind
to your burning lips

3.
flower holds at bay
butterfly's rough overtures
craves kiss of dewdrop

4.
trees seduced by wind
drop inhibitions shed clothes
I grab a jacket

Limericks

1.

There once lived a man on the Rhein
Who drank endless glasses of wine
He was once so tipsy
He said <*yes*> to a gypsy
When she asked <*Is your wallet now mine?*>

2.

There once was a girl from Havana
Who loved to flaunt her bandana.
When it flew away
She chased it night and day
Till she found she'd arrived in Savannah.

3.

There once was a man from Seoul
Who sat atop a shaky pole
When he fell on his head
They thought he was dead
Till he asked for ice cream in a bowl

4.

There once was a man from Trier
Who drank endless mugs of beer.
Then his rotund belly
Began to shake like jelly
And his pants split in two in the rear.

IV

Intertwined
    (Triolet)

There's something about a rainbow
That reminds me of my first love
My face lights up, my tears flow
There's something about a rainbow.
Time and again he let me know
Sunshine and rain are hand in glove
There's something about a rainbow
That reminds me of my first love.

Enigmatic Union

You are a satellite
orbiting the earth
in outer space
looking for new data,
exploring the unknown.

I am a squirrel
digging the ground,
looking for nuts
I've hidden in places
known only to me.

We are at opposite ends
of the speech spectrum:
one prodigal,
the other miserly
in the use of words

Sometimes it seems a mystery
how, despite our differences
we are still together
moving forward
like two hands of a clock.

Cell Replacement

Twenty years ago beneath
a star studded sky
on that enchanted isle,
time stood still.
While you heaped compliment
upon compliment on me
and thanked me for accepting
your marriage proposal,
I closed my eyes in absolute bliss.
You put your arms around me.
I heard you say,
<*Oh, Honey! You're the best*>
And then ever so gently
you kissed me.

Last night beneath a star studded sky
on that same enchanted isle,
your cell phone rang.
While you heaped compliment
upon compliment on your Business Manager
and thanked him for promoting
your marketing proposal,
I closed my eyes in absolute disgust.
You put your arms around me.
I heard you say,
<*Oh, Harry! You're the best*>
And then ever so gently
you kissed the cell phone.

Lonely Leaf's Lament

Drunk with the adulation
I received from every quarter
while I preened myself
I paid no heed to your
admiring looks.
Seduced by his overtures
I let the treacherous wind
sweep me off my feet and
do a pirouette with me
before he unceremoniously
dropped me to the ground.

You wanted to
pick me up, nurture me,
preserve my beauty
between the pages
of your coveted scrapbook.

I played hard to get
moving away from you
each time you wanted to touch me.
The cruel wind tricked me again,
carried me to dizzying heights,
flirted with me for a while,
and then abandoned me
in an alien land.

Wallowing in this dirty pond
separated in time and space
from where we first met
wasting away
waiting for death
with no one to shed
a tear for me
I dream of the immortality
I might have enjoyed
were I in your possession.

Silent Treatment

There was a time when
we could read
each other's minds.
No need for words
one knew exactly what
the other had to say.
Eloquent silence!

Then came a time when
it was not clear what
the other had in mind.
Words flew in every
direction until we
were verbally bankrupt.
Enforced silence!

At the present time when
it matters little what
the other has in mind,
words seem devoid
of meaning.
Much is left unsaid.
Elective silence!

V

Batting for Bats

A mere mammal
you are a freak.
A cross between
an animal and a bird
you are embarrassed
by your looks.
You are afraid of ridicule.
That is why you make yourself
invisible to the world
hanging upside down
on high perches
during the day
and flying out at night
when the whole world sleeps.

Yet, it is *your* battiness
that inspired the radar.
It is *you* I thank
each time I fly
to distant lands
and make
a safe landing.

Role Reversal

Bottom of the barrel,
residue left behind in cups
worthless individuals at
the rock bottom of society.
These are images that
come to mind when
people talk of dregs.

Strangely, there is one place
I know where dregs
occupy the top position
from which they look down
in contempt on
the prized liquid
at the bottom
seemingly saying,
<*What would you be worth
if we hadn't let you
trickle down through us?*>

Hierarchy is turned on its head
in a coffee maker.

In the Shadows

In the enormous kitchen of
the five star hotel
she slogs day in and day out
to pander to the palates of
the rich and the famous.
Today her assignment is to
create a humongous salad,
the centerpiece of the banquet.
Occupying an entire counter is
the freshest produce sourced from
the best gourmet stores in the land.

A daunting task!

She gets down to business right away.
Chop, slice, grate, dice
Grate, dice, chop, slice
Chop, slice, grate, dice
Grate, dice, chop, slice.
When it is all done,
a good four hours later,
she makes a quick dash
to the fast food joint
for her staple lunch of
burger, fries and soda.

Then begins the process of assembling
the differently shaped fruit and
vegetable pieces on a gigantic platter.
Another four hours' job!
Finally, she inserts tiny gleaming slivers
of red, green and yellow peppers in
strategic places of her chef d'oeuvre
with the precision of a master craftsman
setting rubies, emeralds and topaz in
an expensive piece of jewelry.
<Perfecto> she says under her breath
admiring her handiwork.
Her boss gives a condescending nod.

It's time to leave.
As she puts away
her apron and bonnet
she espies her boss posing
behind *her* masterpiece,
getting photographed.

Unperturbed she rushes home
to her one room shack and
watches her favorite soap opera.
For dinner she warms up
a store bought frozen pizza
in her microwave oven.

Transmutation

I've turned from a genius
into a moron.
I'm a mother.

When I answered the *hows* and *whys*
of a school kid,
it was, <*Oh! Mummy, you're a genius*>.

Then came a time when,
intimidated by the computer
it was *my* turn to ask
the *hows* and *whys*.
And the reaction was:
<*But Mom, this is so user friendly.
Why don't you get it*>?

Now, all my *hows* and whys
get a standard answer:
<*Mom, forget it. You won't understand it*>.

I've turned from a genius
into a moron.
I'm a mother.

Reflections

I go to the ocean to still my mind
while I watch the waves and listen
to their unfailing rhythm as they
rise and fall and then come rushing
to caress my feet.

Some rise higher than the others before
they splash down.
Then each one runs with all the strength
it can muster to reach the beach.
Was it the waves that inspired
the motto of the Olympic Games
Citius, Altius, Fortius?

I think it matters little
which wave rises higher
which one reaches the beach first
or which one runs the farthest.
Their energy spent, they all retreat
only to be buried under
the new oncoming waves
that repeat the pattern.

From somewhere I hear
<*Punarapi jananam, punarapi maranam*
Punarapi janani, jathare shayanam>*

My mind set on an even keel
I retreat.

---

*Again and again we are born, again and again we die
Again and again we return to the mother's womb
from *Bhaja Govindam*, a composition in Sanskrit by
the 8th century Hindu philosopher Adi Shankaracharya.

Insidious Changes

No matter the place of manufacture,
no matter the quality of fabric,
they don't make T-shirts
the way they used to.

Earlier, I looked and felt the same
in every T-shirt that I wore
no matter whether new or old,
no matter the quality of fabric
or the place of manufacture.

Now, every time I wear a T-shirt
whether new or old,
I pull and stretch it in every direction
all to no avail.
The old ones have either shrunk
or lost their shape,
the new ones are badly tailored,
and the result is always the same.
I end up looking like
an overfilled sausage.
They just don't make T-shirts
the way they used to.

What has gone wrong?

Suddenly I remember my father's advice
on packing:
<When you overstuff a bag, it loses its shape>

So, now I get it!
It's not the T-shirts that are at fault.
The real culprit is the stuffing!

Cutting Edge Technology

The liquid ruby on my finger
converts itself to soft garnet
before morphing
into solid onyx.

I marvel at the miracle
wrought by
the kitchen knife.

Glimmer of Hope

Traveling to Trenton on the R 7 *,
dreary, desolate, depressing scenes:
boarded buildings, gross graffiti,
abandoned automobiles, ghastly garbage,
once thriving communities gone to seed.

Suddenly, a burst of color!

A small cluster of trees
bedecked in full fall finery,
filling me with hope
that I may yet find
a redeeming feature
in your dark and sinister nature.

* R 7 The South Eastern Pennsylvania Transport Authority train that runs between Philadelphia, PA and Trenton, NJ

Layers

I ask myself if I should accept you whole
with your designer clothes and charming accent
like Brussels sprouts in béchamel sauce
at a fancy restaurant,
unaware of what may be lurking
under the multiple layers.

For, when at home I hold the sprouts under water,
that witch Suspicion raises her ugly head,
and as I peel and discard layer upon layer
finding a black spot here and a brown spot there
I begin to wonder
what blemishes lie beneath *your* layers.

While I can throw away the tainted parts of the sprout,
what do I do when I find your tarnished side?
Ignore it? Pretend it doesn't exist?
Should I continue to delve deeper
with the hope of finding something
wholesome inside?

What if I discover you're rotten to the core?
Would I have the courage to dump you
as I would a rotten sprout?

A scary thought!

They say what you don't know doesn't hurt…..
Was ich nicht weiss, macht mich nicht heiss

I think I will accept you whole
with your designer clothes and charming accent
like Brussels sprouts in béchamel sauce
at a fancy restaurant.

NETWORKING
(Reflections on Bubble Pond in Acadia National Park, Maine)

Raindrops fall on Bubble Pond
Some collapse on contact,
turn into ripples.
Others transform themselves
into bubbles
hope to survive without help
on the surface.
Most find the struggle daunting
give up and opt to become ripples
too, joining the others to form
a large network.
Their belief in the adage
<If you can't beat them, join them>
saves their day.

The larger and prouder bubbles ,
fiercely entrepreneurial, don't give up.
Impervious to the fast approaching
predatory network, they continue
to outdo each other while competing
with the mountain close by
that bears their name.
Sadly, in their quest for upward mobility,
they grow horizontally
rather than vertically
before finally falling flat
on their faces.

Someone should have told them
Bubble Mountain is itself a product
of networking.

Looking Back

Unable to swallow the whole capsule
the old man cuts it open and empties
its contents in a glass of orange juice.

Once a champion jockey, known simply
as CJ, he never lost a single race and
left the arena in a blaze of glory.

Now he recollects his last race. His only
threat at the time was a youngster,
the nephew of a former rival.

Although it was his first time on *that*
race track the young man had won
several trophies overseas.

All who watched him during practice
were filled with awe. No one doubted
he would be the winner of this race.

At the starting line on that important day,
the young man said he felt queasy, blamed
it on the orange juice he was given.

He was far ahead of CJ at the start
but half way through the race
he fell off his horse.

The crowd roared as CJ won the race
by several lengths.   Newspapers called him
The Undisputed King of the Race Track.

Old man CJ now confined to his wheelchair
begins to feel queasy. He flings the untouched
glass of orange juice at the wall.

Dust to Dust

Mined in Africa, polished in Europe,
set in precious metal in Asia,
you had adorned my finger for years.

Suddenly one fall afternoon
in the mountains of New Hampshire
you decided to part company with me.
I cried when I saw the gaping hole in the ring.
How could you have been so cruel?
Hadn't I taken good care of you over the years?
What was going to be your fate now?
You would get trampled upon and be buried
in dirt and slime.
What an awful resting place for one
who was used to a velvet bed
when not sparkling on my creamy finger!

I cried some more.

Clarity returned after a period of numbness.
I realized you had something to tell me.
You had been snatched from your abode
and treated with various degrees of cruelty
just like the people who worked on you,
only to fill the coffers of the handlers
and pander to the vanity of the likes of me.
Had anyone paid attention to *your* tears
or those of the hapless workers?

Yes, you poor thing! You had had enough
and decided to make a quiet exit.
As you fell to the ground, I imagined
the falling leaves in brilliant colors
of ruby, emerald and topaz
conspiring to weave a blanket for you,
and a little later, the older ones tucking you
in a garnet comforter.
I felt relieved.

Good 'bye my little sparkler!
I hope you are happy where you are.

Stirring the Pot

As I watch the vegetable pieces
in different shapes, colors and textures
bobbing up and down,
competing with each other
in the furiously boiling water,
I am filled with doubt.
Will they ever come together
to form a cohesive whole?
I stir the pot.

A little later I find the earlier rivalry
replaced by a spirit of cooperation.
The pieces have softened,
are now in close proximity
to each other.
The water has absorbed
the colors they have shed.
I stir the pot again.

After a while I see the pieces
have made further adjustments
to form a group
while retaining their individuality.
I add some spices
and stir the pot.

I turn off the heat
let the contents sit for a while.

I stir the pot one last time
and taste the concoction.
It is delicious.
I marvel at the unification
of disparate ingredients.

From somewhere I hear
   E Pluribus Unum

www.ingramcontent.com/pod-product-compliance
Lightning Source LLC
LaVergne TN
LVHW041555070426
835507LV00011B/1103